Happy
Birthday!

To

_____

From

_____

Date

_____

Happy Birthday!

hugs
eXpressions of the Heart™

Happy Birthday!

HOWARD BOOKS
A Division of Simon & Schuster

NEW YORK LONDON TORONTO SIDNEY

Our purpose at Howard Books is to:
- *Increase faith* in the hearts of growing Christians
- *Inspire holiness* in the lives of believers
- *Instill hope* in the hearts of struggling people everywhere

Because He's coming again!

Published by Howard Books, a division of Simon & Schuster
1230 Avenue of the Americas, New York, NY 10020

Happy Birthday! © 2006 by Howard Books

ISBN 13: 978-1-58229-561-9
ISBN 10:   1-58229-561-1

10 9 8 7 6 5 4 3 2 1

HOWARD is a registered trademark of Simon & Schuster, Inc.

Manufactured in China

For information regarding special discounts for bulk purchases, please contact Simon & Schuster Special Sales at 1-800-456-6798 or business@simonandschuster.com.

Contributors: Angie Kiesling, Chrys Howard, Debbie Webb, Philis Boultinghouse
Edited by Philis Boultinghouse
Cover design by Terry Dugan Design
Interior design by Stephanie D. Walker

Contents

Blessing

Imagination

Restoration

Tapestry

Home

Dramatics

Adventure

Youthfulness

CHAPTER 1

Blessing

On this day, however many years ago, God gave a gift to the world. That gift was you. There's no one else quite like you. The way you laugh. The way you smile. That special way your eyes light up. The combination of talents that makes you uniquely you.

Did you ever stop to think that in some way, either big or small, your life touches every person with whom you come in contact? Today, on your birthday, let that human "touch" be a return blessing—a thank-you note to God for the gift of life he gave you. As you bless others, you'll be surprised to find how often good things drop into your own lap.

BELIEVING HEAR,
WHAT YOU DESERVE TO HEAR:
YOUR BIRTHDAY
AS MY OWN TO ME IS DEAR . . .
BUT YOURS GIVES MOST;
FOR MINE DID ONLY LEND
ME TO THE WORLD;
YOURS GAVE TO ME A FRIEND.

Martial

LIFE HAS NO BLESSING
LIKE A PRUDENT FRIEND.

Euripides

• Birthdays Are for Giving •

When Marjorie passed her fortieth birthday, she began to realize that birthdays were not always a welcomed celebration. But she had come to value them more and more in the last five years. It had been five years since her diagnosis of breast cancer. Five years since she'd had surgery. Five years since she'd begun a frightening year of chemotherapy. Five years since she'd discovered the importance of a perfectly matched wig and the fun of wearing fancy hats. Five years since she had told her children that there might not be another birthday celebration in her future. But the chemo and surgery had done their appointed jobs, and Marjorie thanked God daily that she was still celebrating birthdays. Never again to complain about the aging process, only grateful to be aging at all!

This birthday was to be a very special one. In celebration of five cancer-free years and the fact that she was turning fifty, her husband had offered to send her and her two daughters to a famous spa in California. It would afford her every relaxation a woman could imagine. She planned to take full advantage of the exercise program as well as spend a day getting a facial and massage. She imagined herself coming back home with brightly colored toenails and a "California" hairdo. Marjorie felt as if her life were just beginning, and she was ready to jump in with both feet!

The day of the trip arrived, and Marjorie joined her two daughters on the airplane headed for luxury. They were shocked to find that the travel agent had not been alert enough to make sure they were seated together, but they took it in stride, and Marjorie sat five rows behind her excited daughters. She decided that the relaxation process would begin on the plane and that she would quietly enjoy a book. One of the lessons she had learned in the last five years was that she rather enjoyed her own company.

After carefully tucking away her purse and fastening her seat belt, Marjorie opened her book to chapter 7, ready to immerse herself in the drama of a good John Grisham novel. *What a great birthday present*, Marjorie thought. *I really do deserve a week of focusing on myself.* No sooner had this thought passed through her mind than a woman about her age stood beside her. "Excuse me," she said. "I'm in the window seat."

"Of course," said Marjorie, unfastening her seat belt and

standing in the aisle. Marjorie didn't mind that someone would be sitting beside her, but now she would have to be friendly, and she preferred just to be quiet.

Marjorie and her new travel companion fastened their seat belts and pretended not to notice each other for about three minutes—but this was not like Marjorie, and she soon introduced herself. She found out that her seatmate's name was Elaine and that she was going to San Diego.

"San Diego," Marjorie said. "I am too. My husband is sending my daughters and me to a spa for my fiftieth birthday." Marjorie conveniently left off her cancer story. She'd been defined by cancer long enough.

"How exciting," Elaine responded, her eyes focused on her hands. "I wish I could say my trip had a great surprise at the end. But I'm afraid I've already gotten my surprise, and it wasn't so great."

Sensing despair in her new friend's voice, Marjorie asked if there was anything she could do.

"I don't think so," she replied. "You see, my daughter was just diagnosed with breast cancer, and I'm on my way to help her as she begins her treatment."

Marjorie quietly closed her book, knowing that sometimes birthdays are for giving and not just for getting.

Praise the LORD,
O my *soul*,
and forget NOT
all his *benefits*.

Psalm 103:2

Blessing

Imagination

Restoration

Tapestry

Home

Dramatics

Adventure

Youthfulness

CHAPTER 2

Imagination

Birthdays. The more you have, the more likely you are to say "Ho hum" when the big day rolls around. After all, you've been here before—maybe more times than you care to remember. But your birthday is special. It's the only day of the year that you can call your own. Why not give your imagination free rein today? Take the time to indulge in a mini mind-safari. You may be surprised at the places you "go" in the next twenty-four hours!

If you're feeling really adventurous, try whipping up a dream "to do" list. Let your imagination go wild. Then make at least one item on your list come true. Try for two or three.

WHAT LIES AHEAD OF YOU
AND WHAT LIES BEHIND YOU
ARE NOTHING
COMPARED TO WHAT LIES
WITHIN YOU.

Author Unkown

● Imagination Station ●

What do you imagine
Is the best birthday treat?
Would a chocolate cake with shiny candles
Make your day complete?

Or do you need a clown or two
On a cake that's strawberry red
And friends to come and spend the night
But never go to bed?

Is pin the tail on the donkey
A game you like to play?
Or would you rather bowl or skate
To celebrate your day?

Or does your imagination
Include a beach house and a book
While someone serves you dinner
That you didn't have to cook?

Go ahead, you decide;
Choose what you want to do.
That's what birthdays are all about—
Celebrating you!

Chrys Howard

Come and *see* what
God has DONE,
how *awesome*
his *works* in
man's behalf!

Psalm 66:5

Blessing

Imagination

Restoration

Tapestry

Home

Dramatics

Adventure

Youthfulness

CHAPTER 3

Restoration

Birthdays are a great time to recharge your battery. If you work, ask for the day off (some companies grant birthdays as automatic holidays) and squander the time with the relaxation activity of your choice: a day at the beach, reading in a shady park, flopping on the couch, enjoying professional beauty services—the list is only limited by your imagination. Or schedule a tête-à-tête with your spouse, a good friend, or God. (He always keeps appointments.)

God set the divine pattern for rest and relaxation when he created the world then stopped to admire his handiwork and rest on the seventh day. Today is a good day to store up your reserves, enjoy favorite memories, and feed your spirit.

HAPPY
BIRTHDAY!

When one finds company
in himself and his pursuits,
he cannot feel old,
no matter what his years may be.

A. B. Alcott

Nothing gives rest but the sincere search for truth.

Blaise Pascal

• Flowers for Marcie •

Large, silent tears slid down Marcie's cheeks. How would she make it through this day?

As if on cue, Stephanie appeared at Marcie's office door. "Hey, birthday girl, what's wrong? You're not that old."

Marcie tried to meet her friend's eyes with a brave smile, but when she saw the compassion in her eyes, she dissolved into tears again.

"I was thinking about Allen," she said between sobs. "This is my first birthday without him. He always did this special thing . . . and, well . . . I miss him."

"I know you do," Stephanie said assuringly. "Look, in thirty minutes it'll be time for lunch—and I promised to treat you for your birthday, remember?"

"I haven't forgotten," Marcie said, the first hint of a real smile on her face. "Thanks."

Marcie turned back to her computer and her many unanswered e-mails. But she couldn't focus. The words swam as her eyes teared up again. Her thoughts returned to that day—more than thirty years ago—when Aunt Margaret had told her and little Allen that both her parents had been killed in a car accident. Aunt Margaret and Uncle James had raised her and Allen as their own children. But their lives never were the same.

It was the little things that hurt most, like remembering her father's tradition of giving her roses for her birthday, one for every year. The first time—her fourth birthday—Daddy had come home with four roses, each a different color. Her mother had put them in a white vase and set them on Marcie's dresser. They were just like the flowers Daddy gave Mommy for her birthday. Best of all, she got to smell and touch them all she wanted.

He'd done the same thing on her fifth and sixth birthdays. No matter what other gifts she got, the roses from her daddy were always her favorite.

On her seventh birthday—the first without her parents—Marcie had cried the whole morning, aching for the white vase filled with colorful roses on her very own dresser.

Only when Allen had padded over to the bed and sat beside her did her sobbing slow. "Marcie, please tell me what's wrong."

"I'm crying because I miss Mommy and Daddy—

especially today because it's my birthday. Daddy used to bring me roses—one for each year old I was." She had smiled at the memory. "He'd get as many colors as he could find. Today he would have brought me seven roses. Mommy would have put them in a white vase in my room so I could touch and smell them all I wanted." She sniffled. "I miss that. Do you understand?"

Allen had nodded somberly and laid his head on Marcie's shoulder.

Grown-up Marcie forced herself to read the e-mail on her screen. But halfway through her first memo, Marcie's mind returned to her seventh birthday.

Aunt Margaret had given her a wonderful party. But after the cake was eaten, the friends had gone home, and the presents were put away, Marcie had gone to her room and closed the door. She'd gotten everything but the one thing she wanted most.

That was when Allen came in with his hand behind his back. "I got you a present, Marcie—like Daddy." With that, he'd held out a fistful of flowers—seven in all. Some were weeds from the field behind Aunt Margaret's house, and some were flowers from neighbors' yards. "I couldn't find any roses," Allen had said cautiously, "but they're all different colors. Maybe Aunt Margaret will let us use one of her flower holders."

"They're perfect!" Marcie had squealed. "This is my favorite present of all!"

She would never forget Allen's beaming face. After that, Allen had always given her flowers for her birthday—one for every year and as many different colors as he could find. As he'd gotten older and had money of his own, he'd started buying roses—just like their dad.

On the eve of her last birthday, Stephanie had helped Allen get into her office after hours and fill it with forty-one roses—in every available color—in big, white vases.

But three months after that birthday, Aunt Margaret had once again been the bearer of bad news. Allen had been killed in a convenience-store robbery. He'd been at the wrong place at the wrong time. Now he was gone—the last member of her immediate family, her last real link to Mom and Dad.

Marcie was jolted back to the present when Stephanie stuck her head in the door. "Hey, girl, it's time to go! Ready?"

At the restaurant the hostess led the two friends through rows of tables to a back room. As they entered, a loud "Surprise!" stopped Marcie in her tracks. All her coworkers were gathered around a festive table with a beautifully decorated cake in the center. Beside the cake were several gifts. Marcie was truly pleased at the thoughtfulness of her friends and colleagues.

As they walked back into the office building, Marcie hugged Stephanie. "Thank you for the wonderful surprise; it was just what I needed."

"I'm so glad," Stephanie replied with a squeeze. "Enjoy the rest of your day."

As Marcie approached her office door, a familiar fragrance filled the air. It was the smell of her father, the smell of her brother; it was the smell of roses. She opened the door and was greeted with a visual delight. White vases filled with roses were everywhere. Two huge arrangements were on her desk, three more on her credenza. Every shelf, every corner—everywhere—overflowed with roses of every color and variety.

"There are 126 roses," Stephanie said from behind her. "Forty-two from your mom, forty-two from Allen, and forty-two from your dad. Happy birthday, sweetie. Your friends love you very much.

"And one more thing: you can smell and touch them all you want."

Take my *yoke* upon you and *learn* from me, for I am *gentle* and *humble* in heart, and you will *find* REST for your souls.

Matthew 11:29

Blessing

Imagination

Restoration

Tapestry

Home

Dramatics

Adventure

Youthfulness

CHAPTER 4

Tapestry

Birthdays are a good time to reflect on your life, take stock of your relationships, inventory your blessings. Those familiar faces you encounter every day—your spouse, your children, your next-door neighbor, the convenience-store clerk—are like individual threads in a beautiful and complex tapestry. You may not see how intricately they are stitched into the pattern of your life for years to come, but they are there just the same.

Take a time-out today to think of all the people who have made your life the rich tapestry it is.

HAPPY
BIRTHDAY!

OUR HAPPINESS DEPENDS ON
THE HABIT OF MIND WE CULTIVATE.
SO, PRACTICE HAPPY THINKING
EVERY DAY. CULTIVATE THE
MERRY HEART, DEVELOP THE
HAPPINESS HABIT, AND LIFE WILL
BECOME A CONTINUAL FEAST.

Norman Vincent Peale

HAPPY BIRTHDAY! HAPPY BIRTHDAY! HAPPY BIRTHDAY! HAPPY BIRTHDAY! HAPPY BIRTHDAY! HAPPY BIRTHDAY! HAPPY BIRTHDAY! HAPPY BIRTHDAY! HAPPY BIRTHDAY! HAPPY BIRTHDAY! HAPPY BIRTHDAY! HAPPY BIRTHDAY! HAPPY BIRTHDAY! HAPPY BIRTHDAY! HAPPY BIRTHDAY! HAPPY BIRTHDAY! HAPPY BIR

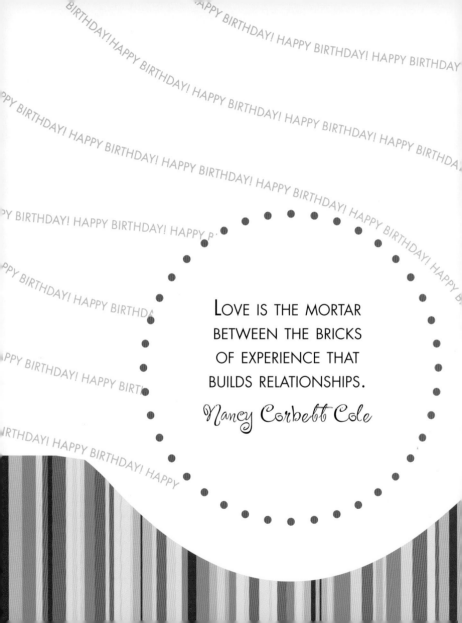

LOVE IS THE MORTAR
BETWEEN THE BRICKS
OF EXPERIENCE THAT
BUILDS RELATIONSHIPS.

Nancy Corbett Cole

• Threads •

Joan stretched like a cat as she climbed out of the car. The long drive back to her childhood home had been a grueling one, but anticipation had made every mile marker trigger another memory. Today many of those memories would assume flesh and blood as she saw again the faces of her aunts, uncles, cousins, and even siblings who had moved too far away for frequent contact. Emily, her six-year-old daughter, would meet many of those relatives for the first time today. And not only was it a family reunion, it was Joan's birthday.

Joan took Emily by the hand and wound her way to the back of the sprawling homestead that belonged to her Uncle Frank and Aunt Edna. The three-story house, older than anyone there, had housed three generations of Beaumonts. Passing through the arbor gate, she saw the gathering of people out back—some faces were familiar; others had completely changed.

After the usual pleasantries, Joan picked up a Styrofoam plate and got in the food line that reached across the shady backyard. Food was always a good icebreaker. Maybe at the picnic table, conversation would flow more easily with these people, who had once been such vibrant pieces of her family puzzle. Now they seemed almost strangers.

"Emily, why don't you try to meet some of your cousins after lunch," Joan encouraged her daughter, who hovered close to her side. Her self-conscious daughter had always found it difficult to make friends. Emily frequently came home from school in tears, the object of other kids' scorn.

"Mommy, why am I different?" she asked her mother as they said their bedtime prayers. It had become a familiar refrain. Speech therapy was helping, but her stutter still surfaced from time to time. Maybe today, among family, things would be different.

"Well, who can this be?" a voice beside her said. Joan glanced up and saw her mother's second-oldest sister, Jane, gazing at Emily. Aunt Jane had always been the odd one of the family. An unusual thread in the family tapestry. She had heard stories about Aunt Jane since her childhood, but she could count on one hand the number of times she had seen her in person.

Aunt Jane had never married. Now she was old—probably dying, some whispered. In her younger days she had traveled to exotic places and written brief letters home about this or that adventure, only to emerge with a different tale in some other exotic place weeks later. She'd show up on relatives' doorsteps on Christmas Eve, then disappear again after the midday meal the next day. "I'm a free spirit," she'd say brightly. "Gotta go where the wind takes me." And off she went—leaving disgruntled family members behind.

But at least Aunt Jane cared enough to make the cross-country flight to attend the family reunion. Most likely, it would be her last. Here she was, surrounded by her immediate family, and yet they seemed to have little to say to her. She felt drawn, instead, to a little girl she'd never met before—a distant grandniece.

"I-I-I'm Emily," the child said gravely as she stared up at the face bent over her. "How old are you?"

"Emily!" Joan scolded, but Aunt Jane laughed and waved off the childish faux pas.

"Don't get upset with her. She has every right to know how old I am," she said, her eyes crinkling at the corners. To Emily she added, "Tell you what—after lunch let me show you something special. If you like it, you can have it when I'm finished. And to answer your question, I'll be seventy-seven on my next birthday."

"Is it pretty?" Emily asked.

"Is what pretty, sweetheart?"

"The surprise," Emily said.

"Oh, yes, it's going to be very pretty indeed."

Mercifully, conversation was lively during lunch, and Joan reconnected with two or three cousins while Aunt Jane talked privately with Emily. After the meal Aunt Jane asked Joan for permission to take Emily to see the surprise. The two slipped away toward the house.

An hour passed.

"Have you seen my daughter?" Joan asked Uncle Frank as he came lumbering down the front porch steps, the screen door slapping behind him.

"Saw her just a minute ago with Jane in the sitting room," he said in his gruff manner. "Whatever they're doing, they're having an awfully good time at it."

Treading lightly down the hall, Joan peeked into the sitting room Aunt Edna had created for "peace of mind" years ago. There, side by side on the flowered sofa, sat Emily and Aunt Jane.

"Those kids don't mean to hurt you," she overheard Aunt Jane say. "They just don't understand you because you're special. You're different from them, but different can be a very good thing. Imagine what a flower garden would look like if all the flowers were the same."

Emily sat quietly beside her great-aunt, taking in her words and watching her work. Aunt Jane's wrinkled hands flew as she worked a needle in and out of an intricate needlepoint on her lap. When the needlework was finished, the fabric would make a beautiful piece of art, suitable for framing.

"You see how tattered it looks from this side?" Aunt Jane said, turning the cloth over. "If you didn't have all these knots and tangled threads here, the top wouldn't look pretty. But when you finish, everything comes out right. It always does in the end."

Joan smiled. Even unusual threads have their place in the tapestry that becomes a family. Without knowing it, Aunt Jane had given Joan a birthday gift she would never forget.

I *praise* you
because I am *fearfully*
and *wonderfully* made.

Psalm 139:14

Blessing

Imagination

Restoration

Tapestry

Home

Dramatics

Adventure

Youthfulness

CHAPTER 5

Home

In *The Wizard of Oz*, a travel-weary Dorothy repeats a phrase that has become synonymous with the famous film: "There's no place like home. There's no place like home. There's no place like home."

And she was right.

Nothing compares with the serenity of home, that place where you not only hang your hat but rest your head and calm your heart. We all need to cocoon once in a while. Being at home gives our physical bodies and our spirits a chance to stoke up for the next foray into life.

HAPPY
BIRTHDAY!

THE ACHE FOR HOME
LIVES IN ALL OF US,
THE SAFE PLACE
WHERE WE CAN GO AS WE ARE
AND NOT BE QUESTIONED.

Maya Angelou

A HOUSE IS MADE
OF WALLS AND BEAMS;
A HOME IS BUILT
WITH LOVE AND DREAMS.

Author Unknown

• Found at Last •

I t was sheer coincidence. Or was it providence? Surely some unseen hand had directed the course of Maura's life these past few months for just such a time as this.

Maura Langley had driven out to the old cemetery on the east side of town to photograph some tombstones for a piece she was doing for the fall issue of *Freedom* magazine. Taking some time off from the local newspaper because of office politics, which she felt stifled her creative abilities, Maura was freelancing for a year and enjoying some freedom of her own. At least, as long as her finances would sustain her.

Maura truly was independent, though not by choice. Her mother and father had been killed in a car accident when she was three years old, leaving her to be reared by an aunt on her mother's side. Her only sibling, a sister, had been delivered by the emergency medical technicians at the scene of the accident and adopted by a hopeful couple in a nearby town. She and her sister had never met. And in spite of her efforts, Maura had been unsuccessful in tracking down any information about her.

The dusty gravel road wound around to the entrance of the graveyard and ended at the gate where Maura parked her 1998 Honda Civic. Maura knew this cemetery well and parked in her usual spot. She noticed another vehicle parked to the side of the road, tipped sharply to the passenger's side on the steep embankment. Her mind registered a minor irritation at the possibility of an intruder. She rarely saw visitors here. Why today, when she needed to work?

Maura grabbed her camera case, two rolls of film, and a half-empty bottle of water that had accompanied her most of the day. With long, brisk strides, she headed into the heart of the cemetery, stopping to use a large concrete crypt as a table for her setup. Adjusting the wide-angle lens for her first shot, Maura caught a slight movement in the top right-hand corner of the frame. Her eyes darted instinctively to the spot, zooming in on what appeared to be a solitary picnic very near a familiar grave.

Lowering her camera, Maura strained to confirm with naked eyes what she'd seen through the lens. There sat a young woman on a blanket near a grave. Her hand gestures suggested that she was conversing. But she was alone.

Maura snapped a few shots and worked her way across

the lawn to observe the young woman at closer range. Sure enough, there in front of her own parents' graves, an attractive, dark-haired woman sat eating sandwiches and talking to the Langleys' tombstones. Maura couldn't help but notice a small cake that seemed to occupy a prominent placement in the center of the blanket. It seemed odd to her that there was a candle in the cake.

"Excuse me," Maura ventured. The young woman gasped with surprise. In her preoccupation with her picnic, she hadn't seen Maura coming. "I apologize for interrupting you," Maura continued, "but I'm curious as to why you would be eating a picnic in a cemetery all alone."

"Oh, I do this every year on this date."

"Really?" Maura mused. "Well, you might find this an interesting coincidence. You've chosen to have your picnic with my parents this year. Tom and Sheila Langley. They died in a car wreck twenty-six years ago, and I'm their daughter Maura. They are buried right beside where you're sitting."

The young woman involuntarily dropped both her sandwich and her jaw. Coughing and sputtering as the color drained from her cheeks, she struggled to speak. Maura moved toward her with a reassuring gesture, hoping to relieve her apparent embarrassment: "It's OK with me, and I'm sure they appreciate the company."

The young woman rose to her feet, asking breathlessly, "Do you know what today's date is?"

"August 28," Maura replied.

The dark-haired stranger motioned for Maura to come closer as she moved toward the headstone. Her fingers ran across the date of death etched in granite as her eyes watched for Maura's expression. "August 28," Maura read, "the day my parents died."

Tears welled up in the young woman's eyes and poured over onto her delicate cheeks as she continued. "Today is my birthday. That is why I'm here. I have been coming here since I was sixteen to celebrate my birthday with my parents. You see, I was born on the day my mother and father died in a car wreck twenty-six years ago. I never met them, but I'm their daughter Mattie."

Intense emotion gripped Maura's heart as her mind wrestled to adjust to the implications of the facts she'd just been presented. This was her sister—her long-lost sister—whom she'd never met. Instinctively and longingly, they searched each other's faces for recognition. And as if on cue, the two sisters ran into each other's arms and wept in an unforgettable embrace until the torrent of tears had passed. Maura and Mattie Langley had found each other in the only spot on the earth—a burial plot—that tied them together.

"Oh, Maura," Mattie sobbed, "I never knew I had a sister. No one ever told me. I've felt so alone my whole life," she continued. "Year after year I've come here on the anniversary of our parents' deaths and my birth. It has always been such a sad day for me. But this was to be my last. I had come to say good-bye. You see, I'm getting married next month and will be moving to the West Coast. What if you hadn't been here today? I'd have never known you in this life."

Maura touched her baby sister's face with a tender hand. She felt a familiar ache inside for the absence of memories of growing up together: telling secrets, playing dolls, giggling over boys. But a bittersweet consolation swept over her heart. "Mattie, I've experienced another kind of loneliness all these years. You see, I knew I had a sister, and I have grieved so long over losing you. But now my grief is gone. I have found you at last."

The sun set that August day on two sisters sitting together at a significant grave site, sharing peanut-butter sandwiches, a birthday cake, and the stories of their separate lives. The setting of that summer sun marked the dawning of a future together as a family. Forever changed, their histories now merged into a legacy of love that would last their lifetimes and generations to come.

He will *rise* up
and *restore* your
happy *home.*
And though you
started with *little,*
you will *end* with
MUCH.

Job 8:6–7 NLT

Blessing

Imagination

Restoration

Tapestry

Home

Dramatics

Adventure

Youthfulness

CHAPTER 6

Dramatics

Remember when you were a kid and your birthday was the biggest day of the year? Well, maybe it played a reluctant second fiddle to Christmas, but inside, it was the event you secretly waited for. The calendar pages never seemed to turn so slowly as when you approached the final countdown of weeks and days until your birthday.

Birthdays were a time for high drama. Lavish cakes. Streamers and balloons. Party dresses. Pomp and circumstance.

Today, why not turn back the clock and get dramatic again? Have some creative fun with your birthday festivities. Whether you've been hankering for a new hair color or a try at skydiving, now's the time to go all out.

HAPPY
BIRTHDAY!

THERE WAS NEVER YET
AN UNINTERESTING LIFE.
SUCH A THING IS AN IMPOSSIBILITY.
INSIDE OF THE DULLEST EXTERIOR
THERE IS A DRAMA, A COMEDY,
AND A TRAGEDY.

Mark Twain

• The Drama Queen •

I am the drama queen,
Or so I've been told
By friends and family close to me
Who say that I'm too bold.

And, yes, I often dress quite strange.
I say I have a flair
For dressing better than the rest
With flowers in my hair.

Most of the year my antics are few,
I try to keep them quiet,
But on my birthday, I just let loose,
They say that I'm a riot!

After all, it's just one day—
It's my birthday, time to cheer!
And then I'll chill and settle down
Until this time next year!

Chrys Howard

The *heavens* tell of the GLORY of *God.* The *skies* display his marvelous *craftsmanship.* Day after day they *continue* to SPEAK; night after night they make *him known.*

Psalm 19:1–2 NLT

Blessing

Imagination

Restoration

Tapestry

Home

Dramatics

Adventure

Youthfulness

CHAPTER 7

Adventure

Life is an adventure, whether we sign on for the ride or not. At times it's like a roller coaster, at other times like bumper cars, and—mercifully—some days breeze by like glider swings. However they're spent, our days on this earth pass by in an ever-quickening haze of activity. If we're not careful, we can miss the view from the top. And it's those momentary glimpses of glory that make it all worth the effort.

On your birthday make every minute count. Don't just seize the day; seize the second. Go out of your way to mark this day with adventure. Reach out and grab the brass ring!

You'll always be glad you did.

AGE I make light of it,
FEAR not the sight of it,
TIME'S but our playmate,
whose toys are divine.

Thomas Wentworth Higginson

ADVENTURE
IS WORTHWHILE.

Amelia Earhart

• The Greatest Gift •

Maryanne Scott had seen the commercials that advertise a popular arthritis treatment. "I don't want to climb a mountain," the woman on the commercial says. "I just want to play a game with my grandchildren." But Maryanne did want to climb a mountain. It was the one adventure she had never had the opportunity to pursue, and now that she was almost seventy, she felt time was running out. If she didn't do it this year, she was afraid it would take more than that arthritis medicine to get her to a mountaintop.

Maryanne's love for the mountains began many years earlier when she and her husband took annual family ski trips to Colorado. Sunny Florida was a great place to live—and she wouldn't trade it for anything—but the mountains called her back every winter for at least two weeks of skiing.

Always athletic, Maryanne and her husband, Bill, loved bringing family and friends to the mountains to share their enthusiasm for the winter sport.

But her sweet husband had been gone almost five years now, and Maryanne knew that he was the reason she wanted to climb a mountain. He had often commented that he'd love to visit Colorado in the summer to see what the mountains looked like without the snow. But two of their four grown children lived out of state, and for some reason they always wanted to come home during the summer! Maryanne and Bill couldn't very well be gone when their children were home.

But now an opportunity to climb a mountain had arrived. Maryanne's granddaughter was going to Colorado with her church youth group. Maryanne was a little apprehensive about asking her granddaughter if she could tag along, but she couldn't help herself. This was her last chance!

Three months before the trip, Maryanne invited her granddaughter Cassie to lunch. "Cassie, please don't think I'm a crazy old fool, but I have something important to ask you," Maryanne said in a very sheepish voice.

"What is it, Mamaw? You can ask me anything. You want to know why kids today pierce their eyebrows?" joked Cassie.

"That's a good question, but not the one I have for you today," Maryanne responded. Then she continued, "I have already asked your youth minister, but now I need to ask you. Would you mind if I went on the mountain climb with your youth group? I've always wanted to climb a mountain, and this could be my last chance. My birthday is during the week of the climb, and I would love to turn seventy on the top of a mountain. Wouldn't that be a great celebration?"

Cassie looked at her grandmother as if she had just asked her if she could go with her on a trip to the moon. Actually, a trip to the moon may have seemed more reasonable. At least on the moon, gravity wouldn't be a factor, and her grandmother wouldn't fall flat on her face. The spacecraft would certainly be easier on her mamaw than three days walking up a steep mountain. Cassie had made this mountain climb the year before and knew the dangers and difficulties involved.

But Cassie cleared her head of her doubts and looked straight into her grandmother's eyes. "You bet you can go. I would love to spend a week with you on the mountain," Cassie said as she reached across the table to give her a hug. Cassie had always been close to her grandmother and was truly excited about the added adventure this would bring, but she wasn't so sure how the rest of the teenagers would take it. *I'll cross that bridge later*, she thought. *My grandmother is pretty cool. They'll see.*

The weeks following that conversation were filled with excitement as Maryanne and Cassie worked together to prepare for the trip. They developed a walking program designed to build up Maryanne's stamina and a weightlifting program that would ensure that Maryanne could carry her backpack. Maryanne was determined to carry her share of the load each day of the journey, and since she had always kept herself in good shape, she felt pretty confident in her ability to make it to the top successfully.

The day arrived for nineteen teenagers and six sponsors to board a bus and begin their adventure. Maryanne had already elected not to join the teens for this part of the trip. She knew the bus ride would be long, and she needed to save her energy for better things. *After all, at sixty-nine, surely I'm allowed some compromises*, she had reasoned. So two days earlier she had flown to the nearest Colorado town and was resting comfortably in a hotel room as a very noisy busload of "brave babes," as Maryanne called them, trekked across America. Maryanne could just imagine them laughing and talking loudly with a set of earphones in every teen's ears. *It would have been fun, but right now a good night's sleep is more important*, she thought as she turned off the lamp in her hotel room. *I'll see the kids soon enough.*

Soon enough did come, and Maryanne was surprised to find that she was slightly nervous as she waited for the bus to arrive. She couldn't help but notice the stares of the young mountain crew when she announced that she would be making the trip with the youth group that would arrive that day. *That's OK*, she thought, *it's my birthday, and I'll do whatever I want to celebrate it! I'll bet some of these young 'uns will climb a mountain when they turn seventy too. They just can't imagine it now!*

The bus did arrive, and things began to move very quickly. After hugs and introductions all around, the preparation began. Each person was issued a backpack; each four-person team, a tent; and each cooking group, portions of the daily meals. Maryanne's backpack was at least ten pounds heavier than she had anticipated. As she bent down to the ground to see if there was anything she could leave, three big boys from her group volunteered to carry some of her load. Maryanne protested, but the young men insisted, and she soon realized that helping each other was a big part of what this mountain climb was all about.

As it turned out, Maryanne witnessed countless acts of kindness—not just toward herself, but toward all of her fellow adventurers. She witnessed one boy carry a girl's backpack for five hours after she injured her foot on a loose rock. She watched in almost disbelief as two other young men carried this same young woman to the top so she wouldn't be left behind. Maryanne listened as words of encouragement flowed from the mouths of these "babes," encouraging her and others to continue on and make it to the top. She thanked God as she soaked up the words of her travel companions, so much younger than she, who offered up prayers for strength and courage.

On Maryanne's seventieth birthday, she celebrated—as she had planned—on the top of a mountain. The view was breathtaking, just as she had imagined for so many years. She cried as she "talked" to her husband about the journey she had just taken, wanting to share it with him in some small way. Then she praised God for his majesty and thanked him for the best birthday gift he could have ever given her.

"My great and glorious God, I thank you for the beauty of this day and creation you have given us. As I look across these mountains, I marvel at a sky so blue that I am drenched in its color and a lake that looks as if a master painter weaved the best of his palette in every delicate stroke. I am reminded of the song 'How Great Thou Art' and want to sing it at the top of my voice. But, dearest God, now that I've made this journey, I know that this glorious view is not really the greatest gift I've received on this, my seventieth birthday. No mountain, sky, or lake could equal the inspiration, encouragement, and support that these nineteen teenagers have given me this week. That's the best birthday gift I could ever ask for. And I know you knew it all along. Thank you for giving more than I could ask or imagine."

This is the *day* the *LORD* has *made.* We will REJOICE and be *glad* in it.

Psalm 118:24 NLT

HAPPY
BIRTHDAY!

AN ADVENTURE IS ONLY AN
INCONVENIENCE RIGHTLY CONSIDERED.
AN INCONVENIENCE IS ONLY AN
ADVENTURE WRONGLY CONSIDERED.

G. K. Chesterton

HAPPY BIRTHDAY! HAPPY BIRTHDAY! HAPPY BIRTHDAY! HAPPY BIRTHDAY! HAPPY BIRTHDAY! HAPPY BIRTHDAY! HAPPY BIRTHDAY! HAPPY BIRTHDAY! HAPPY BIRTHDAY! HAPPY BIRTHDAY! HAPPY BIRTHDAY! HAPPY BIRTHDAY! HAPPY BIRTHDAY! HAPPY BIRTHDAY! HAPPY BIRTHDAY! HAPPY BIRTHDAY!

Blessing

Imagination

Restoration

Tapestry

Home

Dramatics

Adventure

Youthfulness

CHAPTER 8

Youthfulness

Youth has very little to do with age and much to do with state of mind. Whatever marker your birthday celebrates this year, take a moment to remember some of the symbols of your youth:

- running barefoot through the prickly grass
- catching lightning bugs in a jar with a friend
- recording your heart's secrets in your diary
- riding a bike for the very first time

Now, take that same spirit and apply it to some new adventure you've been leery of trying or a secret you've not yet ventured to realize. You really can do it—for youthfulness is a state of mind.

YOU CAN'T HELP
GETTING OLDER,
BUT YOU DON'T HAVE TO
GET OLD.

George Burns

ONE CAN NEVER
CREEP WHEN
ONE FEELS
AN IMPULSE TO SOAR.

Helen Keller

• Something More •

Mom, puh-leeeeze," Lauren groaned, her eyes rolling. The mall would close in fifteen minutes, and her mother, Beverly, was desperately seeking a new skirt. With time running out, she was forced to try an old trick her sister had taught her. She held the skirt to her front and wrapped it from side to side to see if the seams lined up with the outside of her legs. Then she held it to her backside and did the same. Beverly knew that mirrors and seams never lied.

"We would like to inform all shoppers that the doors will close in fifteen minutes," the voice over the loudspeaker said. Lauren was thrilled. She had shopped all her twelve-year-old body could shop. Besides that, Lauren was always a bit embarrassed by her mother's unconventional behavior. Beverly knew her daughter had to put up with a lot from her. Their personalities were direct opposites. Lauren was quiet and laid back, just like her daddy. Beverly, on the other hand, sang along with songs on the car radio with the windows down. She often requested extra chocolate chips in her scoop of chocolate chip mint from puzzled teenagers behind the counter at the local ice-cream shop. And worst of all, she drove Lauren to school in her bathrobe. "Who would ever know?" her mother reasoned. Lauren had made her promise never to get out of the car.

But today was Beverly's birthday, and Lauren was trying to be as patient as she could with her mother, who had a few years earlier decided that she wanted to stop growing up. "I don't mind growing older," she would say, "I just don't want to grow up." Celebrating her birthday always included something "goofy," as Lauren put it.

Lauren had decided to try being a little "goofy" herself to help her mom celebrate her thirty-fifth birthday. It wasn't easy for a "non-goofy" kid to be "goofy," but she did have a plan.

Once they got home from the mall, Lauren told her mom to go put on some jeans and a sweatshirt. As Beverly returned from her bedroom, she noticed Lauren putting something in her pocket.

"Follow me," Lauren ordered, and they headed behind their house to a hill that overlooked a canyon. Lauren's head moved back and forth as if she were searching for a buried treasure. Soon she said, "This is the place. Sit right here. It might be a little damp, but we'll be OK."

"OK, this is a great place," Beverly replied and plopped down Indian style next to her daughter. "Now what?"

Fifteen minutes of silence passed while the sun sank lower in the sky. Together, mother and daughter watched as gold fused into pink and, finally, purple. There on the side of a little hill, they shared a sunset. At that moment, Lauren took a bottle out of her pocket and blew bubbles toward the horizon. Beverly watched each bubble emerge as they shimmered and floated against the sky.

"Now make a wish," Lauren said quietly. "Happy birthday, Mom."

Beverly was filled with love for a daughter whose nature would be to put candles on a cake but whose love told her she needed to do something more.

HAPPY
BIRTHDAY!

GOD'S GIFTS PUT MAN'S BEST
DREAMS TO SHAME.

Elizabeth Barrett Browning

HAPPY BIRTHDAY! HAPPY BIRTHDAY! HAPPY BIRTHDAY! HAPPY BIRTHDAY! HAPPY BIRTHDAY! HAPPY BIRTHDAY! HAPPY BIRTHDAY! HAPPY BIRTHDAY! HAPPY BIRTHDAY! HAPPY BIRTHDAY! HAPPY BIRTHDAY! HAPPY BIRTHDAY! HAPPY BIRTHDAY! H

Those who *hope* in the LORD will *renew* their *strength*. They will *soar* on wings like EAGLES; they will *run* and not grow weary, they will walk and *not* be *faint*.

Isaiah 40:31

Express
YOURSELF!
Show how much you *care*
with these *heartfelt* books from the
BEST-SELLING HUGS™ LINE

Get Well!—ISBN: 1-58229-563-8
Thanks! —ISBN: 1-58229-562-X
Way to Go!—ISBN: 1-58229-564-6

HOWARD BOOKS
A DIVISION OF SIMON & SCHUSTER
NEW YORK LONDON TORONTO SIDNEY

Available where good books are sold.

Happy Birthday!